Shakespearean Sallies, Sullies, and Slanders

Shakespearean

Sallies, Sullies, and Slanders

Insults for All Occasions

Collected by Ann McGovern

Illustrated by James and Ruth McCrea

Thomas Y. Crowell Company / New York

By the Author

Robin Hood of Sherwood Forest

Shakespearean Sallies, Sullies, and Slanders:
    Insults for All Occasions

The text for this book follows *The Oxford Shakespeare*. Capitalization and line division have been altered in a few instances.

Here are a few of the unpleasant'st words
That ever blotted paper.

— *The Merchant of Venice,* III, ii

Contents

Short and stinging,

or

Every word stabs

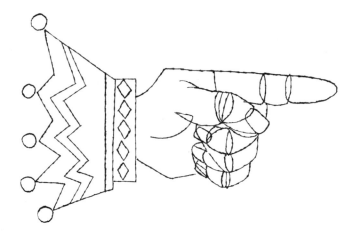

Thou stool for a witch!

—*Troilus and Cressida,* II, i

Thou art a wickedness.

—*Twelfth-Night,* II, ii

The south-fog rot him!

—*Cymbeline,* II, iii

Thou crusty batch of nature.

—Troilus and Cressida, V, i

Thou disease of a friend.

—Timon of Athens, III, i

Your misery increase with your age!

—Coriolanus, V, ii

The dropsy drown this fool!

—The Tempest, IV, i

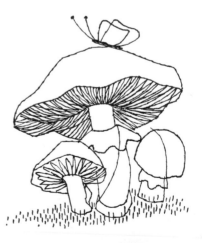

4

Pernicious blood-sucker of sleeping men.

—Henry VI, Part II, III, ii

O, gravel heart!

—Measure for Measure, IV, iii

Every word stabs.

—Much Ado About Nothing, II, i

Death is too soft for him.

—The Winter's Tale, IV, iii

Something wicked this way comes.
　　　　　　　　　—Macbeth, IV, i

Blasts and fogs upon thee!

—King Lear, I, iv

A pox o' your throats!

—Measure for Measure, IV, iii

Poison be their drink!

—Henry VI, Part II, III, ii

Vengeance rot you all!

—Titus Andronicus, V, i

For fatties,

or

O! that this too too solid flesh would melt

She is spherical, like a globe. I could find out countries in her.
—*The Comedy of Errors,* III, ii

A plague of sighing and grief! it blows a man up like a bladder.
—*Henry IV, Part I*, II, iv

O! that this too too solid flesh would melt.
—*Hamlet*, I, ii

Ye fat-kidneyed rascal!
—*Henry IV, Part I*, II, ii

Thou clay-brained guts.
—*Henry IV, Part I*, II, iv

Huge hill of flesh.
—*Henry IV, Part I*, II, iv

Stuffed cloak-bag of guts.
—*Henry IV, Part I,* II, iv

Bolting-hutch of beastliness.
—*Henry IV, Part I,* II, iv

Swoln parcel of dropsies.
—*Henry IV, Part I,* II, iv

Sweats to death, and lards the lean earth as he walks along.
—*Henry IV, Part I,* II, ii

13

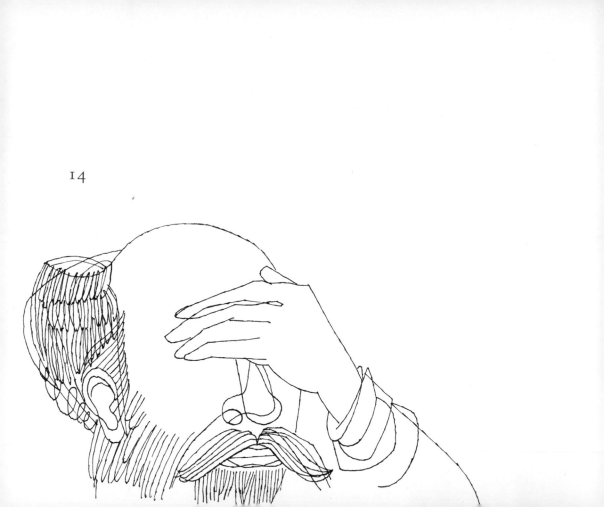

Ugly as sin,

or

His face is the worst thing about him

I have seen better faces in my time than stands on any shoulder that I see before me at this instant.

—King Lear, II, ii

Foul wrinkled witch.

—Richard III, I, iii

God hath given you one face, and you make yourselves another.

—Hamlet, III, i

They have the plague, and caught it of your eyes!
—*Love's Labour's Lost,* V, ii

His face is the worst thing about him.
—*Measure for Measure,* II, i

The tartness of his face sours ripe grapes.
—*Coriolanus,* V, iv

God made him, and therefore let him pass for a man.
—*The Merchant of Venice,* I, ii

Thou paper-faced villain.

—*Henry IV, Part II*, V, iv

I never can see him but I am heart-burned an hour after.

—*Much Ado About Nothing*, II, i

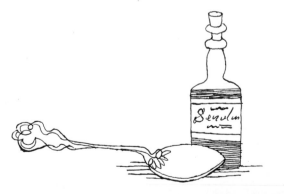

For someone you never want to see again,

or

Let's meet as little as we can

Unbidden guests are often welcomest when they are gone.
—*Henry VI, Part I,* II, ii

I do desire we may be better strangers.
—*As You Like It,* III, ii

Let's meet as little as we can.
—*As You Like It,* III, ii

23

If I hope well, I'll never see thee more.
—Timon of Athens, IV, iii

We know each other well.
We do, and long to know each other worse.
—Troilus and Cressida, IV, i

I dote on his very absence.
—The Merchant of Venice, I, ii

Direct thy feet where thou and I henceforth may never meet.
—Twelfth-Night, V, i

Go thou and fill another room in hell.
>   —*Richard II*, V, v

I thank you for your company; but, good faith, I had as lief have been myself alone.
>   —*As You Like It,* III, ii

26

Cutting words,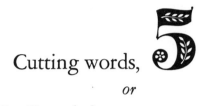

or

I will speak daggers

She would infect to the north star.

—*Much Ado About Nothing,* II, i

I will speak daggers to her.

—*Hamlet,* III, ii

I could endure anything before but a cat, and now he's a cat to me.

—*All's Well That Ends Well,* IV, iii

28

If he were opened, and you find so much blood in his liver as will clog the foot of a flea, I'll eat the rest of the anatomy.
—*Twelfth-Night*, III, ii

There is the man of my soul's hate.
—*Coriolanus*, I, v

Bloody, bawdy villain! Remorseless, treacherous, lecherous, kindless villain!
—*Hamlet*, II, ii

If thou hast no name to be known by, let us call thee devil!
—*Othello,* II, iii

May his pernicious soul rot half a grain a day.

—Othello, V, ii

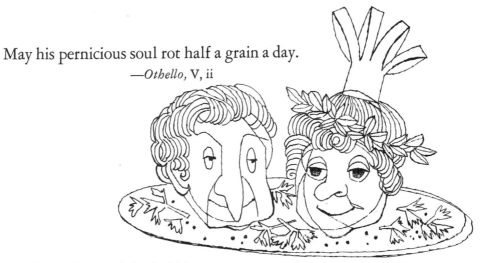

Let their vile heads be bak'd.

—Titus Andronicus, V, ii

Let worse follow worse, till the worst of all follow him laughing to his grave.
—*Antony and Cleopatra*, I, ii

Let vultures vile seize on his lungs.
—*Henry IV, Part II*, V, iii

Make him by inch-meal a disease.
—*The Tempest*, II, ii

For a two-faced friend,

or

One may smile, and smile, and be a villain

34

You lie, up to the hearing of the Gods.
                    —*Antony and Cleopatra,* V, ii

His treasons will sit blushing in his face.
                    —*Richard II,* III, ii

Hide not thy poison with such sugar'd words.
                    —*Henry VI, Part II,* III, ii

O! wonderful, when devils tell the truth!
—*Richard III,* I, ii

If thou speak'st false, upon the next tree shalt thou hang alive,
till famine cling thee.
—*Macbeth,* V, v

36

Thou art all ice, thy kindness freezes.
                    —*Richard III,* IV, ii

There's neither honesty, manhood, nor good fellowship in thee.
                    —*Henry IV, Part I,* I, ii

38

Fic, fic! you counterfeit, you puppet you!   39
    —*A Midsummer-Night's Dream,* III, ii

He that depends upon your favours swims with fins of lead
and hews down oaks with rushes.
    —*Coriolanus,* I, i

I will no more trust him when he leers than I will a serpent
when he hisses.
    —*Troilus and Cressida,* V, i

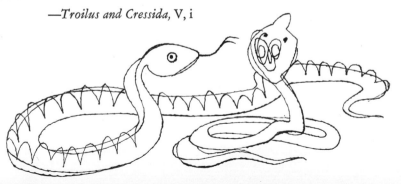

One may smile, and smile, and be a villain.
—Hamlet, I, v

One day he gives us diamonds, next day stones.
—Timon of Athens, III, vi

If I prove honey-mouth'd, let my tongue blister.
—The Winter's Tale, II, ii

He waxes desperate with imagination.
—Hamlet, I, iv

A blister on his sweet tongue.

—Love's Labour's Lost, V, ii

The devil can cite scripture for his purpose.

—The Merchant of Venice, I, iii

There's no more faith in thee than in a stewed prune.

—Henry IV, Part I, III, iii

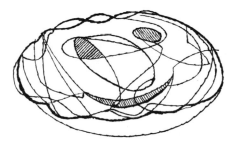

For a cry-baby,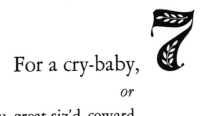

or

Thou great-siz'd coward

Go, prick thy face, and over-red thy fear, thou lily-liver'd boy.

—*Macbeth,* V, iii

That great baby you see there is not yet out of his swaddling-clouts.

—*Hamlet,* II, ii

Go, lest I let forth your half-pint of blood.

—*Coriolanus,* V, ii

44

He has strangled his language in his tears.
—*Henry VIII,* V, i

They have only stomachs to eat and none to fight.
—*Henry V,* III, vii

Thou great-siz'd coward.
—*Troilus and Cressida,* V, x

He would drown the stage with tears.
—*Hamlet,* II, ii

46

On your way,

or

Vanish like hailstones; go

Go, ye giddy goose.

—Henry IV, Part I, III, i

Farewell, you muddy knave.

—Henry IV, Part I, II, i

Take thy face hence.

—Macbeth, V, iii

Out, dog! out, cur! thou driv'st me past the bounds
of maiden's patience.
>   —*A Midsummer-Night's Dream,* III, ii

Vanish like hailstones; go.
>   —*The Merry Wives of Windsor,* I, iii

Out of my sight! thou dost infect mine eyes.
>   —*Richard III,* I, ii

Go; vanish into air; away!
>   —*Othello,* III, i

Hie thee to hell for shame, and leave this world.
>   —*Richard III,* I, iii

Go shake your ears.
>   —*Twelfth-Night,* II, iii

Out, you green-sickness carrion! Out, you baggage!
You tallow face!
>   —*Romeo and Juliet,* III, v

Away you scullion! you rampallian! you fustilarian!
I'll tickle your catastrophe.
—Henry IV, Part I, II, i

Away! Thou'rt poison to my blood.
—Cymbeline, I, i

Out, you mad-headed ape!
—*Henry IV, Part I,* II, iii

Fellow, be gone! I cannot brook thy sight.
—*King John,* III, i

I will deal in poison with thee . . . I will kill thee a hundred and fifty ways: therefore tremble, and depart.

—*As You Like It*, V, i

Hence, rotten thing! or I shall shake thy bones out of thy garments.

—*Coriolanus*, III, i

Go; get you home, you fragments!

—*Coriolanus*, I, i

Polluted air,

or

My nose is in great indignation

The rankest compound of villanous smell that ever offended nostril.

—*The Merry Wives of Windsor,* III, v

Would thou wert clean enough to spit upon!
—*Timon of Athens,* IV, iii

A very ancient and fish-like smell.
—*The Tempest,* II, ii

56

My nose is in great indignation.
>   —*The Tempest,* IV, i

You are smelt above the moon.
>   —*Coriolanus,* V, i

She sweats; a man may go overshoes in the grime of it.
>   —*The Comedy of Errors,* III, ii

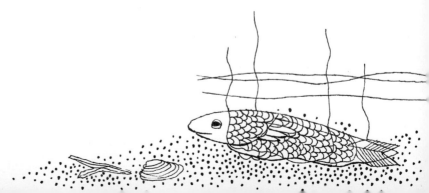

Devastating dialogues,

or

I know what I know.
I can hardly believe that,
since you know not what you speak.

I'll beat thee, but I should infect my hands.
I would my tongue could rot them off!
—*Timon of Athens,* IV, iii

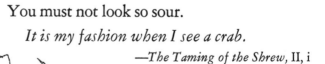

You must not look so sour.
It is my fashion when I see a crab.
—*The Taming of the Shrew,* II, i

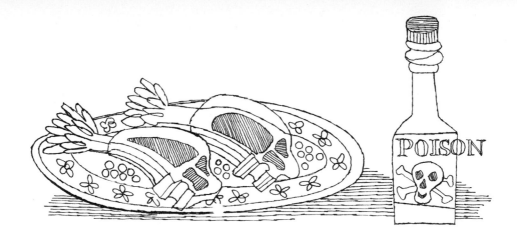

Would poison were obedient and knew my mind!

Where wouldst thou send it?

To sauce thy dishes.

—*Timon of Athens,* IV, iii

When I know not what else to do, I'll see thee again.
When there is nothing living but thee, thou shalt be welcome.
—Timon of Athens, IV, iii

Give me your hand and let me feel your pulse.
There is my hand and let it feel your ear.
—The Comedy of Errors, IV, iv

I know what I know.
I can hardly believe that, since you know not what you speak.
—Measure for Measure, III, ii

Curses on curses,

or

A plague on thee! thou art too bad to curse!

The peril of our curses light on thee so heavy as thou shalt not shake them off.

—King John, III, i

Take with thee my most grievous curse.

—Richard III, IV, iv

My tongue will tell the anger of my heart.

—The Taming of the Shrew, IV, iii

64

O thou, well skilled in curses, stay awhile,
And teach me how to curse mine enemies.
—*Richard III,* IV, iv

My hair doth stand on end to hear her curses.
—*Richard III,* I, iii

Can curses pierce the clouds and enter heaven?
Why then give way quick clouds to my quick curses.
—*Richard III,* I, iii

A plague on thee! thou art too bad to curse!
    —*Timon of Athens,* IV, iii

If there be Devils would I were a Devil,
To live and burn in everlasting fire,
So I might have your company in hell,
But to torment you with my bitter tongue!
    —*Titus Andronicus,* V, i

Some devil whisper curses in my ear,
And prompt me, that my tongue may utter forth,
The venomous malice of my swelling heart!
> —*Titus Andronicus,* V, iii

The curses he shall have, the torture he shall feel, will break
the back of man, the heart of monster.
> —*The Winter's Tale,* IV, iii

Help me curse that bottled spider, that foul bunchback'd toad.
> —*Richard III,* IV, iv

Sophisticated slanders,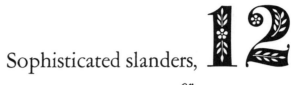

or

In his sleep he does little harm

There is no more mercy in him than there is milk
in a male tiger.

—*Coriolanus,* V, iv

A goodly apple rotten at the heart.

—*The Merchant of Venice,* I, iii

Many a good hanging prevents a bad marriage.

—*Twelfth-Night,* I, v

Smacking of every sin that has a name.
    —Macbeth, IV, iii

He may keep his own grace, but he's almost out of mine.
    —Henry IV, Part II, I, ii

There's small choice in rotten apples.
    —The Taming of the Shrew, I, i

In his sleep he does little harm.
    —All's Well That Ends Well, IV, iii

The devil himself could not pronounce a title more hateful to
mine ear.

—*Macbeth*, V, vii

When you're mad enough to start throwing punches,

or

By this hand, I will supplant some of your teeth

I'll slit the villain's nose.

—The Taming of the Shrew, V, i

I had as lief thou didst break his neck as his finger.

—As You Like It, I, i

I will beat thee into handsomeness.

—Troilus and Cressida, II, i

Guard thy head; for I intend to have it ere long.
—*Henry VI, Part I,* I, iii

I will inflame thy noble liver, and make thee rage.
—*Henry IV, Part II,* V, v

I will not answer thee with words, but blows.
—*Henry VI, Part I,* I, iii

By this hand, I will supplant some of your teeth.
—*The Tempest,* III, ii

76

I'll unhair thy head: Thou shalt be whipp'd with wire, and stew'd in brine, smarting in lingering pickle.

—Antony and Cleopatra, II, v

Here by the cheeks I'll drag thee up and down.

—Henry VI, Part I, I, iii

I will grind your bones to dust.

—Titus Andronicus, V, ii

I'll have this secret from thy heart, or rip thy heart to find it.

—Cymbeline, III, v

The smallest thread that ever spider twisted from her womb
will serve to strangle thee.
—*King John,* IV, iii

80

The female tongue,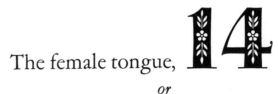

or

The cruell'st she alive

Paint till a horse may mire upon your face: A pox of wrinkles!
—*Timon of Athens,* IV, iii

And though she be but little, she is fierce.
—*A Midsummer-Night's Dream,* III, ii

She chide as loud as thunder when the clouds in autumn crack.
—*The Taming of the Shrew,* I, ii

She is an irksome, brawling scold.

> —*The Taming of the Shrew,* I, ii

Lady, you are the cruell'st she alive.

> —*Twelfth-Night,* I, v

Her beauty and her brain go not together.

> —*Cymbeline,* I, ii

Two women plac'd together makes cold weather.

> —*Henry VIII,* I, iv

84

I'll have thy beauty scratch'd with briers.

—*The Winter's Tale*, IV, iii

No devil will fright me then so much as she.

—*Love's Labour's Lost*, IV, iii

Could I come near your beauty with my nails
I'd set my ten commandments in your face.

—*Henry VI, Part II*, I, iii

Comb your noddle with a three-legg'd stool.

—*The Taming of the Shrew*, I, i

You play the spaniel, and think with wagging of your tongue
to win me.

—*Henry VIII,* V, iii

That kiss is comfortless as frozen water to a starved snake.

—*Titus Andronicus,* III, i

I am not yet so low but that my nails can reach unto thine eyes.

—*A Midsummer-Night's Dream,* III, ii

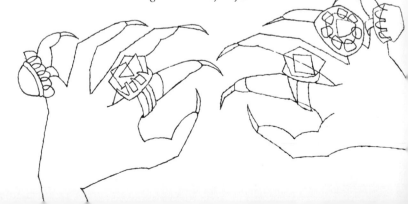

For a fool,

or

Little little less than little wit

I was seeking for a fool when I found you.
—*As You Like It,* III, ii

Gross lout, a mindless slave.
—*The Winter's Tale,* I, ii

You heedless joltheads and unmanner'd slaves!
—*The Taming of the Shrew,* IV, i

88

Wears his wit in his belly, and his guts in his head.
—Troilus and Cressida, II, i

Beetle-headed, flap-ear'd knave!
—The Taming of the Shrew, IV, i

Idol of idiot-worshippers.
—Troilus and Cressida, V, i

Better a witty fool than a foolish wit.
—Twelfth-Night, I, v

He has not so much brain as ear-wax.

—*Troilus and Cressida,* V, i

Thou full dish of fool.

—*Troilus and Cressida,* V, i

Your wit makes wise things foolish.

—*Love's Labour's Lost,* V, ii

Thou hast no more brain than I have in mine elbows.

—*Troilus and Cressida,* II, i

He's winding up the watch of his wit; by and by it will strike.
—*The Tempest,* II, i

You blocks, you stones, you worse than senseless things!
—*Julius Caesar,* I, i

Thou hast pared thy wit o' both sides, and left nothing i' the middle.

—*King Lear,* I, iv

There's many a man hath more hair than wit.

—*The Comedy of Errors,* II, ii

You souls of geese, that bear the shapes of men.
—*Coriolanus,* I, iv

Wilt thou show the whole wealth of thy wit in an instant?
—The Merchant of Venice, III, v

His wit is as thick as Tewksbury mustard.
—Henry IV, Part II, II, iv

That little little less than little wit.
—Troilus and Cressida, II, iii

Thou mongrel, beef-witted lord!
—Troilus and Cressida, II, i

For a bore, **16**

or

Bethump'd with words

Well said: that was laid on with a trowel.
—*As You Like It,* I, ii

Thrust those reproachful speeches down his throat.
—*Titus Andronicus,* II, i

'Zounds! I was never so bethump'd with words.
—*King John,* II, i

Here will be an old abusing of God's patience and
the king's English.
                    —*The Merry Wives of Windsor,* I, iv

Harp not on that string.
                    —*Richard III,* IV, iv

You cram these words into mine ears, against the stomach of
my sense.
                    —*The Tempest,* II, i

Have your mouth fill'd up before you open it.
—Henry VIII, II, iii

They have been at a great feast of languages, and stolen the scraps.
—Love's Labour's Lost, V, i

O! they have lived long on the alms-basket of words.
—Love's Labour's Lost, V, i

She does abuse our ears.
—All's Well That Ends Well, V, iii

More of your conversation would infect my brain.

—*Coriolanus,* II, i

Why should she live, to fill the world with words?

—*Henry VI, Part III,* V, v

Will not a calf's-skin stop that mouth of thine?

—*King John,* III, i

As tedious as a twice-told tale, vexing the dull ear
of a drowsy man.

—*King John,* III, iv

Speaks an infinite deal of nothing, more than any man.
>—*The Merchant of Venice*, I, i

Talk thy tongue weary.
>—*Cymbeline*, III, iv

Here's a fellow frights humour out of his wits.
>—*The Merry Wives of Windsor*, II, i

Cease thy counsel, which falls into mine ears as profitless as water in a sieve.
>—*Much Ado About Nothing*, V, i

I hear a tongue, shriller than all the music.
—*Julius Caesar,* I, ii

Stop his mouth, and let him speak no more.
—*Titus Andronicus,* V, i

Thy words are blunt, and so art thou.
—*Henry VI, Part II,* IV, i

When you want to have the last word, **17**

or

I leave you, sir, to the worst of discontent

I'll haunt thee like a wicked conscience.
          —Troilus and Cressida, V, x

A silly answer and fitting well a sheep.
          —The Two Gentlemen of Verona, I, i

Were I like thee I'd throw away myself.
          —Timon of Athens, IV, iii

107

You are as a candle, the better part burnt out.
—*Henry IV, Part II,* I, ii

You are not worth the dust which the rude wind blows
in your face.
—*King Lear,* IV, ii

Thou'rt so leaky, that we must leave thee to thy sinking.
—*Antony and Cleopatra,* III, xi

Asses are made to bear, and so are you.
—*The Taming of the Shrew,* II, i

A fiend like thee might bear my soul to hell.
—Twelfth-Night, III, iv

Henceforth be never number'd among men!
—A Midsummer-Night's Dream, III, ii

Thou canst make no excuse current, but to hang thyself.
— *Richard III,* I, ii

You'll be rotten ere you be half ripe.
—As You Like It, III, ii

110

You will hang like an icicle on a Dutchman's beard.
>   —*Twelfth-Night,* III, ii

You are not worth another word.
>   —*All's Well That Ends Well,* II, iii

I wish you all joy of the worm.
>   —*Antony and Cleopatra,* V, ii

Go, suck the subtle blood o' the grape, till the high fever
seethe your blood to froth.
>   —*Timon of Athens,* IV, iii

Tempt not too much the hatred of my spirit, for I am sick when I do look on you.

—*A Midsummer-Night's Dream,* II, i

Thou call'dst me dog before thou hadst a cause, but, since I am a dog, beware my fangs.

—*The Merchant of Venice,* III, iii

I do hate thee worse than a promise-breaker.

—*Coriolanus,* I, viii

Thou art a boil, a plague-sore, an embossed carbuncle, in my corrupted blood.

—*King Lear,* II, iv

The most infectious pestilence upon thee!

—*Antony and Cleopatra,* II, v

A vengeance on your crafty wither'd hide!

—*The Taming of the Shrew,* II, i

I leave you, sir, to the worst of discontent.

—*Cymbeline,* II, iii

Thou slander of thy mother's heavy womb! Thou loathed
issue of thy father's loins! Thou rag of honour!
—*Richard III,* I, iii

A south-west blow on ye, and blister you all o'er! 115
—*The Tempest,* I, ii

About Ann McGovern

A performance of *Coriolanus* in Central Park started Ann McGovern thinking about the wealth of vigorous and comical abuse to be found in Shakespeare. As she reread the plays, she discovered more and more — this book is the result.

Mrs. McGovern lives in "The Narrowest House," once the home of the poet Edna St. Vincent Millay, in New York's Greenwich Village. She has written more than a dozen books, a movie for children, and short stories for adults. She has reviewed and edited children's books, as well as producing children's records.

About the Illustrators

Ruth McCrea was born in Jersey City, New Jersey. Her husband is a native of Peoria, Illinois. They both attended the Ringling School of Art in Sarasota, Florida, and took night classes at New York University and at the Brooklyn Museum. Mr. and Mrs. McCrea each grew up with an interest in writing and drawing. Since they met in art school, they have been working together on jacket design, writing, and illustrating. Mr. McCrea has also done book design and, for several years, taught typography at Cooper Union in New York City. Mrs. McCrea has illustrated many books on her own.

The McCreas, who have a son and two daughters, live in Bayport, New York.